Natalie McGrath

The Beat of Our Hearts

Salamander Street

PLAYS

First published in 2022 by Salamander Street Ltd.
(info@salamanderstreet.com)

The Beat of Our Hearts © Natalie McGrath, 2022

ISBN: 9781914228636

10 9 8 7 6 5 4 3 2 1

The Beat of Our Hearts premiered at Exeter Northcott Theatre from 3rd – 5th February 2022.

Cast

Valentine	**Rebecca Todd**
Quill	**Elijah W Harris**
Luca	**Frewyn Thursfield**
Dove	**Kieron Jecchinis**

Creative Team

Writer	**Natalie McGrath**
Director	**Scott Hurran**
Designer	**Pete Butler**
Sound Designer and Composer	**Tom Foskett-Barnes**
Lighting Director	**Jamie Platt**
Movement Director	**Sophie Cottle**
Dramaturg	**Josie Sutcliffe**
Dramatherapist	**Wabriya King**

Production Team

Producer	**Naomi Turner**
Production Manager	**Elaine Faulkner**
Stage Manager (On the Book)	**Zoe Fitzgibbon**
Assistant Stage Manager	**Jay Seldon**
Costume Supervisor	**Aly Fielden**
Set Build	**Backdrop Designs**

Access

Audio Describer	**Jonathan Nash**
Audio Describer Assistant	**Harriet Godfrey**
BSL Interpreter	**Catherine Hall**

Script Development Team

Writer	**Natalie McGrath**
Director / Script Development	**Scott Hurran**
Valentine	**Maggie Bain**
Luca	**Tianna Arnold**
Quill	**Zachary Hing**
Dove	**Andrew Macbean**

Academic Team

Project Lead
Postdoctoral Research Associate
Historical Advisor

Wellcome Centre for Cultures and Environments of Health, University of Exeter
Charlotte Jones
Richard Vytniorgu
Fred Cooper

Project Partners

Exeter Northcott Theatre
www.exeternorthcott.co.uk
Intercom Trust
www.intercomtrust.org.uk

Marketing / PR
Marketing and Development Director
Marketing Manager
PR Consultant
PR Consultant
Press & Marketing Officer & Poster Design
Press & Marketing Officer & Poster Design
Illustration / logo design

Kelly Johnson

Laura Van Wymersch
Gillian Taylor
David Burns
Eleanor Fitzpatrick

Ralph Whitehead

Frank Duffy

Exeter Northcott Theatre

We bring people together to create and share extraordinary experiences.

We believe that stories help us understand each other and the world around us, and that live performance has a unique power to reach out and communicate.

We work with artists and communities so that people can tell their stories no matter who they are or where they've come from.

We make events that entertain, provoke, and inspire so that people can connect and share moments they'll never forget.

We are here for the people of Exeter, Devon, and beyond. To create, to connect, to bring joy and change lives.

www.exeternothcott.co.uk

EXETER NORTHCOTT THEATRE

Acknowledgements and thanks

Daniel Buckroyd (Artistic Director, Exeter Northcott); Andy Hunt (CEO, Intercom Trust); Tina Dixon; The Northcott Technical Team, Front of House and Box Office staff; the WCCEH Research Support team (Kate Ellis, Lucy Hodges, Melanie Shaw and Emma Fowler); Professor Mark Jackson; Professor Manuela Barreto; Professor Jana Funke; Sharifa Hashem Al Hashemy; Exeter Arts & Culture; Exeter City of Literature; Exeter Culture; Being Human Festival; Exmouth Pride, who gave us a sense of what it's like to lead an LGBTQ+ platform in a southwest coastal town; all the amazing organisations who were represented in our stalls in the Northcott bar (Exeter Pride; It's All About You Wellbeing; the Exeter University LGBTQ+ Staff Network and Trans and Non-binary Cafe; Exeter Guild and Student LGBTQ+ Society; Bookbag, a local independent bookshop; Intercom Trust; Out And About; OutStories; and Hidayah LGBTQI+); and everyone who generously shared their stories and ideas with us through our events and workshops – particularly Emily Faulkner, Claire, Michelle Miller, Ruby, Monica, M, Sheena Sen, Grey, Alfie Horrill, Jade Varley, Riley Batty, Mitchy, Elliott Ramsey, Maddie, Perrin Hooper, Jord, and Holly. *The Beat of Our Hearts* was funded and supported by the Arts and Humanities Research Council and Arts Council England.

Acknowledgements and thanks

Foreword

Many LGBTQIA+ people in Britain have experienced exclusion and isolation, both historically and in the present day. This can result from explicit discrimination and hostility in family homes, on the street, and from institutions such as our education and healthcare services, as well as a more diffused cultural bias which favours and normalises some thinking, behaving, and being over others. Loneliness is a significant emotional and psychological expression of this marginalisation. LGBTQIA+ loneliness therefore has a long history, as do the relationships and shared spaces that LGBTQIA+ people have built for solidarity, creativity, and care.

Natalie McGrath's *The Beat of Our Hearts* focuses on experiences of loneliness and belonging negotiated by LGBTQIA+ people in the South West of England. As counties such as Devon, Cornwall, and Somerset are predominantly rural, LGBTQIA+ people living there can face additional or heightened challenges associated with a lack of queer visibility, prejudice, and structural inequalities that effectively marginalise a range of identities and experiences. While these are contemporary challenges, they are also ones with long and complex histories. Nevertheless, these regional stories rarely feature on our national arts landscape.

The Covid-19 pandemic and the impact of government-directed lockdowns also exacerbated existing patterns of loneliness and isolation experienced by LGBTQIA+ people, while raising new challenges. A 2020 independent report to the UN General Assembly found that LGBTQIA+ people were scapegoated as 'vectors of disease' during the pandemic. The lockdown also meant that civil organisations supporting LGBTQIA+ rights, whose sources of income already faced increased strain during the pandemic, also experienced decreased access to policy makers because 'LGBT issues' were not considered a priority at that moment. On a personal level, LGBTQIA+ people experienced increased levels of isolation and minimal opportunities to be together, or forge new friendships or relationships.

From this context, *The Beat of Our Hearts* emerges as a testament to the survival (and revival) of queer love and intimacy. While responsive to the events and impact of the past couple of years, Natalie's play is also reflective of years of thinking on the subject of LGBTQIA+ histories of loneliness and belonging, particularly in the South West. As the culmination of a collaborative project, the play is stimulated by a critical mass of research we've conducted into various forms and histories of loneliness and belonging and their pertinence to the South West and its environment, as well as explorations into LGBTQIA+ community divisions and exclusions, and the struggle for recognition, security and comfort.

Natalie's work first came to the attention of the Wellcome Centre for Cultures and Environments of Health at the University of Exeter in 2019, in response to an open call released by the Centre and the Exeter Northcott Theatre. As one of three artists selected to work with us to explore arts-based research approaches, Natalie brought with her many original conceptual and creative ideas around the project's themes, helping us to explore and express our ideas about loneliness in a new way. Her first sketches of what might later be a script or performance felt urgent and exciting. Here she focused on LGBTQIA+ loneliness, describing the significant loss of physical community and queer meeting spaces, the importance of shared knowledges, histories and heritages, and the relationship between loneliness and survival. Her work was politically energised and it resonated with us personally, as well as with our research.

In partnership with local LGBT+ charity, the Intercom Trust, we developed a series of writing workshops with Natalie to explore how experiences of loneliness and belonging in the South West can be expressed through creative practices. Conversations during the workshops ranged widely, from experiences of Section 28 and trans healthcare, to LGBT+ support groups in places of education and the impact of social media on young people's mental health.

Together we shared queer texts and used them as inspiration to develop ideas. A collaborative poetry exercise helped us to think about the places, things, and experiences that make us who we are. We also wrote letters, took photographs, and shared objects which had a personal significance. When invited to compile a manifesto for tackling LGBTQIA+ loneliness in the South West, participants responded thoughtfully and urgently about the areas they felt needed addressing: areas such as healthcare, queer meeting spaces, and access in schools to LGBTQ+ support groups. It would not be an overstatement to say that the workshops are the beating heart of the play. We were honoured with the honesty and thoughtfulness of everyone who joined us. Talking about loneliness isn't easy, but with the support of the Intercom

Trust we found that coming together as a group created a space in which this became easier – an environment of mutual trust, understanding, and empathy. Natalie led these workshops with us, but she also listened deeply, and allowed the sentiments, moods, and themes to inspire her playscript.

At the centre of *The Beat of Our Hearts* are four characters – Val, Dove, Quill, and Luca – whose friendship and willingness to try and understand one another permeates the play. This is a group of friends whose sense of community is shaken by an act of destruction and deceit, and the characters feel it keenly. Theirs is a potentially vulnerable and exposed community, but it is also one that finds a kind of rebirth and optimism through the course of the play. Natalie's depiction of the southern seascape and the playful rhythm of the natural environment is integral here. We see queer potential, but also anguish; the characters feel both deeply attached to and constrained by their home and surroundings by the coast.

Val, described in the playscript as a 'local kick ass head librarian', has a passion for queer history, and it seems significant that a major response to an act of destruction is to build and consolidate a queer archive. While very much contemporary and of their moment, Val, Dove, Quill and Luca are also self-consciously attuned to historical figures now claimed as part of LGBTQIA+ history. Whether this is Oscar Wilde, Hilda Doolittle, Sappho, or Radclyffe Hall, the characters invoke historical imagination as a tool for reviving a sense of community which has been undermined by recent events. As Quill says, 'I used to spend a lot of time hiding and reading in that corner of the library'. Reading builds solidarity.

But it's not just queer books that *The Beat of Our Hearts* celebrates. Other objects are also important. Echoing one of the workshop activities, in which people shared personal items that somehow spoke to their LGBTQIA+ identity, the characters in Natalie's play also reclaim a sense of belonging through talking about things that are precious to them. This is also about inheritance and legacies. The play seems to suggest that meaning and love can be passed to others through things – a pin badge, a t-shirt, a flag – and especially by giving something to someone else. The act of giving symbolises an opening, an act of generosity and a movement from one person to another. There is intimacy here, in the gift of giving, even across distant periods in time.

Importantly, the play does not shy away from tensions. Good drama should always seek to prise open questions in non-intrusive ways, allowing audiences to make up their own mind about what they are seeing. And there are uncomfortable but crucial questions in *The Beat of Our Hearts*. What does community look like for LGBTQIA+ people in the South West? How do we negotiate different, sometimes competing and perhaps exhausting demands on our affections? And perhaps most importantly, how do we absorb and process difficult experiences that seem to shake the core of who we are?

It's been wonderful to work closely with Natalie over the last couple of years, to explore the synergies across our work, and to support (and admire) her writing process. This collaboration has been unusual in its focus on the South West, bringing together different organisations and individuals with diverse perspectives on the local region, and we're proud to finally celebrate it with you.

Dr Richard Vytniorgu (Research Associate) and Dr Charlotte Jones (Project Lead), University of Exeter, February 2022

***

The Beat of Our Hearts is a play about histories. Each of the four characters – Valentine, Dove, Quill, and Luca – pulls with them a life tangled up in time, with moments of joy, pleasure, connection, safety, and care taken – not gifted – from between the teeth of neglect, erasure, or commodification. Dove's grief over the death of his husband is shadowed by an older loss, as a gay man who survived the AIDS crisis; Quill and Luca are closer to the beginning of their lives, at a point where trans and non-binary people are subject to more vitriol and negation than a decade ago, not less. On a theme where liberal assumptions of 'progress' frequently predominate, Natalie goes out of her way to trouble them:

It's messy out there

Rights being eroded

They're facing all kinds of things we didn't.

Her keen and nuanced sense of history is one of the things – aside from and within the breadth and depth of her vision and skill – that makes collaboration with Natalie such a joy, and *The Beat of our Hearts* such an important play. Reading the script for the first time, I started to see the creation of the archive

– prompted by Valentine's discovery of the photograph of Nightingale and Jack – as a mirror to some of our own processes in working towards the play; although doubtless it owes a considerable debt to Natalie's fantastic work queering the collections at Exeter's Royal Albert Memorial Museum. Like Valentine, Dove, Quill, and Luca, we wanted to make something that brought queer people together around the (re)discovery of a long and shared history, creating a community and building something lasting and good. That the characters turn to an archive is not incidental. Recovering a common past is an essential act of celebration, remembrance, and resistance, embedding us more deeply in the world. Isolation from history can be as keen a pain as isolation from others. As Quill puts it, going barefoot in the ocean:

I'd forgotten how to enjoy this vastness

Thanks for inviting me.

Dr Fred Cooper (Historical Advisor), University of Exeter, February 2022

Characters

VALENTINE (VAL)   *she / her, lesbian. Local kick ass head librarian and activist. Mid-forties.*

DOVE   *he / him, gay. Born in 1957 the year the Wolfenden Report was written. Retired nurse.*

QUILL   *he / him, trans, bisexual. Like the feathers of a bird Quill wants to escape, fly away to warmer climes. Almost thirty.*

LUCA   *they / them, non-binary. Trying to find their own light. Almost twenty.*

Setting

Small seaside town in the South West of England. Rural in its vistas beyond the roar of the ocean. It gathers itself up over winter months where the population shrinks and sighs as the dark nights set in. Blossoms again in the Spring when it starts to open up.

In those months it is a coat with its collar turned trying to block out the insistent force of the Atlantic that never tires, never gives up, never stops to pause.

We are never far from this vastness or coastal paths made for walking for remembering for escape.

A local community library is at the heart of the story. Born out of a time when libraries were gifted to communities. So it has a past. A heritage. Many stories in its evolution.

Time

The play takes place over the space of a year.

Notes

A club beat or a beat runs throughout. It has an ambient heartbeat that rises and falls as the play's emotions rise and fall.

To keep the action lively and moving let's not rely on too many blackouts to signify scene or moment changes. Let's think about how the actors are active in these changes and engage in them with an audience. Let's see the theatricality rather than hiding it away as an illusion. It isn't. It's magic.

One

Deep night time when nothing good happens. The taking down of a pride flag. Its destruction. A chilling moment. Cuts the air like a newly sharpened knife. It is over before it has even begun.

The voices that ring out are hollow and fatal all in one go. They bark in pathetic triumph during the act. This isn't boldness. It's heartlessness. Unimaginative as one shade of darkness eludes to another as their moment of victory passes quickly into emptiness.

Then they are gone.

Clouds hide stars. They would not be able to look. It would break their hearts.

A singular voice pierces the night.

Hatred flies in the face of a cool wind
Rainbow colours that once sang
Fluttered / caressed / ignited this big sky
Gone / in the shake of a fist / a flash of fire

Such a fleeting act / one that will last long
Into the distance / cutting across lives lived /
This moment of pride hard won / a small step
Taken / that was cherished / now crushed

This cruelty / so hard to name / to fathom
Will reach in deep / sear its own mark / multiply
Hearts will want to burst / their limits previously
Unknown / before this knocked on their door

Some might feel an ocean roar inside of them
Some may feel it sting / as anger starts to rise /
Sombre in morning light / as words rip / tear /
Linger for too long / hang heavy / damage done

This isn't just another attack / on another day /
In another place / it's not always somewhere else
Sometimes it's just here / laughing on your own

doorstep / waiting to erupt / waiting to begin

Don't look away / it's not okay to look away / not today
We're being attacked / all over the world / we're dying
As the ground from underneath our feet is taken
Until we can no longer see beauty in ourselves

Why does something always have to break / before
Our lives become more visible in the world's eyes /
Why does something always have to break / before
change can be made?

Two

Next day. Early evening in the library. The day is dying before it should.

VALENTINE, QUILL, LUCA *and* **DOVE** *looking dazed and confused. Tears could fall.*

The texture of this moment is brittle. Ready to snap. A thin electrical current holds them together as anger, fracture and disappointment rise.

VALENTINE *is gathering her momentum. Trying to hold on to her emotions. Not wanting anger to hurt an already hurting mood as she shows them what is left of the pride flag.*

VALENTINE: They burnt it

LUCA: That's all that's left?

VALENTINE: It's what the Police didn't take

DOVE: Valentine?

VALENTINE: I kept some

DOVE: Isn't this evidence?

VALENTINE: Couldn't bear to lose all of it

QUILL: It's just a thing

An object

It's replaceable

VALENTINE: You don't mean that?

QUILL: I do

VALENTINE: Quill

QUILL: What?

VALENTINE: It's so much more than that

QUILL: Is it?

VALENTINE: It symbolises who we are

Our Pride

Our work together

QUILL: These symbols

We place so much hope in them

Look at it

All dishevelled

Smelling of burning

They do look at it. Disbelief flooding out of them. It's just a scrap of the flag it once was.

VALENTINE: I'm going to frame it

QUILL: That's crazy

VALENTINE: Let everyone see it

Let them look

Fuck it

Let them all look

See what has happened

Instead of burying it

Pretending it never existed

DOVE: Won't the Police need it?

QUILL: What will they do with it Dove?

Put it in a file

Draw a veil over it

Do nothing

They don't give a damn

LUCA: It's a hate crime

Tension rising like mercury. Acknowledging this hurts them.

VALENTINE: I let the waves crash around me this morning

Stood amidst them as they hit me full force

Stinging my skin

A wildness seeping into my bones

For a moment it soothed

I'm so angry

What do I do with it?

DOVE *tries to bring a softer mood.*

DOVE: You let that soft butch kick ass chief librarian loose

We need her

VALENTINE: She's here

Somewhere

DOVE: Luca

You're very quiet

LUCA: It wasn't hurting anyone

DOVE: It wasn't

QUILL: It hurts only us

That's the point

LUCA: Then who did it?

VALENTINE: We'll fix this

QUILL: Don't make promises you can't keep

VALENTINE: You're right

I promised this would be

Spectacular

That it would bring some unity

QUILL: Well it didn't

DOVE: This isn't your fault

VALENTINE: Did I push too hard?

LUCA: Took us ages

To get this far

Our lives are as valuable as anyone else's

DOVE: This was about being celebrated in our community

Recognised

Respected

QUILL: It was a huge risk

I knew it would provoke some idiot

LUCA: What if it's someone we know?

Silence. Just a wave of silence between them as they register this.

DOVE: What did the Police say?

VALENTINE: Nothing much yet

QUILL: Nothing much ever

VALENTINE: Usual stuff

DOVE: This isn't usual

QUILL: Isn't it?

Why are you all so surprised?

This is the world we live in

Queer and trans folk

Geting attacked

Everyday

We were lucky it was the flag

Not us

DOVE: People can be so cruel

What about the council?

VALENTINE: They're going to issue a statement

LUCA: I'm frightened

To be in town today

I wasn't before

VALENTINE: I'm so sorry Luca

It's a shock

You're in shock

We all are

LUCA: So close to home

QUILL: If it's erupted on our doorstep

Its not going away anytime soon

Air fracturing is an awful sound. A feeling that rises like bile in the pit of a stomach. It's the acidic end of things.

QUILL: In boxing there are rules

They establish an understanding

Respect alongside

the brutality of two people

trying to beat the shit out of one another

This action is below the belt

Beyond rules

It breaks things

that don't need to bc broken

Creates fear in us

The flag established

a pretence for everyone else

that it's safe for us

out on the street

To step out each day

Into the world

That's what's so cruel about it

VALENTINE: Then you better teach me how to box Quill

Started the day wanting to fight

Still do

Let me roll these sleeves up

Raise my fists

I feel like fighting

QUILL: Maybe we need to cool it

Stop meeting for a while

Re-think what we're doing

VALENTINE: What?

QUILL: I need a re-set

VALENTINE: That's what they want to happen

QUILL: Val you're not listening

Just marching on your crusade

It's not mine

VALENTINE: I thought we were a team

QUILL: Oh fuck off Val

This isn't some work development day

This is our lives

DOVE: Anger won't help

VALENTINE: Won't help who?

DOVE: You

VALENTINE: My first reaction was to smash things

Then I realised

Today I don't know the place we live

That's the saddest thing

Or the people living here

DOVE: That's absurd

It'll be one person

A small group

VALENTINE: I want some harmony

Some fucking harmony

Is it too much to ask?

Who did that flag offend?

Why don't they show their faces

Instead of hiding in the night?

Cowards

Moonlight starts to shine luminously in the night sky flooding the library. Interrupting
VALENTINE. *Catches her off guard just in time. Then stars start to form one by one joining the moon's brightness. The evening's thunder is about to clear.*

DOVE: I was ten when the sexual offences act made homosexuality legal
in 1967 between men over the age of twenty-one

Ten

I remember registering it and in particular a word I didn't quite understand

Decriminalisation

I had to ask what it meant

My parents grumbled like earthquakes about it

Changing the subject when they thought I might be listening

Truth was I was always listening

Picking up left over weekly newspapers

Pouring over the pages for anything in print about homosexuality

I just knew I was drawn to it

Thinking

Is that me then?

My father exploded if I dared to ask any questions

We didn't know as much then

Not like now

There was a sense of innocence

Silence accompanied by stereotypes and misunderstandings and fear

There was always fear and looming violence

I wondered then what would happen to me when I was twenty-one

Legally allowed to look at another man

To touch another man

How could I have to wait that long to know who I was?

Well I didn't wait of course

I went to the library to find out as much as I could

We couldn't afford the luxury of books at home

Reading became a diversion

A hidden learning ground

Knowledge became important to me

I went on a bit of mission

Sleuthing my way through obvious clues to wild guesses

My own translations as I got older

More curious

More aware of my own body

Of other bodies around me at school

I started forming this secret history of those who had come before me

Oscar Wilde of course

I was drawn to his plays and reading between the lines

His humour gave me hope

He gave us laughter and sadness and the most heartbreaking accounts of himself and his love for another man as the establishmentwas stripping him of his humanity

Always gets to me when I think about that

I think of him when I am at my lowest

Sat alone in his cell writing words on pages

Words that would one day sing

Be celebrated

How they might have given him hope

In my twenties

A group of gay friends and I went to an all male production of *The Importance of Being Earnest*

In the grounds of this country estate

I can't even remember how we got invited

In the afternoon before the performance we picnicked and swam in the river running through the estate

Bodies shining in summers end sunshine

Reminding me of Duncan Grant's nudes swimming

Oh it was so exciting to see that painting years later

The sky was a deep clear blue

There were candles and fires to light the actors way to the small stage

They just took their time to read the play

This play that I thought I knew

Unfolding before us

Men together in couples in more than couples

Holding hands

Leaning on one another as those glorious words flowed

In the heat of the night

In the distance we could feel something glow

I saw a figure

We all did

It was Oscar

Watching us

Listening to his words being spoken by men who loved men

Tears falling down his face onto the ground

It only lasted a moment

He was there

His spirit at least

Amongst the living

Little did we know what was ahead

The anguish that was before us

Our community

The devastation that would rumble through us all

Take away so many of my friends

Men I had loved

Had danced long into the night with

Gone before our very eyes

Before their time

Before their voices were heard

That reading was the last time we were all together my friends and I

Before our gatherings became funerals and vigils

The guilt some days of being well was also the beginning of me knowing I had to speak up

To be bolder

Do something

I got involved

Campaigned for rights and healthcare

For our dignity

Our humanity

When I met Hugh I fell in love immediately

I knew the world was telling me I wasn't supposed to

I just did and it felt like magic had landed in my bones

I felt free for the first time

After so long hiding in the shadows

He left a hungry cavernous hole in my heart

The rhythms all off now he's gone

Stravinsky rather than Mozart

Banging around in my chest

We were together for over thirty years

Three

Day after the meeting in the library. The day is waking up to a blustery start. It's early.

Sea vista panorama opening up before us. **LUCA** *is sat on a bench staring out to sea letting the wildness seep in as they sketch the horizon. Somewhere a storm is waiting to be whipped into action. To gather up and blow the elements right through us.*

DOVE *arrives. Not a planned meeting.*

DOVE: I love this coastline

Its geology

Reminds me I'm only one tiny particle

A fleck in a wider story

You're up early

Before the crowds

LUCA: I like the light from here

DOVE: Not sure I could live without the sound of the Atlantic anymore

Its wrapped itself around me

Found its way into my heart

Taken away some sorrow

LUCA: It'll do that

DOVE: Fresh morning

You not cold?

LUCA: Nope

    LUCA *makes room for* **DOVE** *on the bench.* **DOVE** *takes up the offer.*

DOVE: Young people

No coats ever

LUCA: Has to be at least six degrees

DOVE: Ouch

I was the same

LUCA: Where are you off too?

DOVE: Gets me out of bed walking along here

New drawings?

LUCA: Constantly evolving with the tides

DOVE: Always different isn't it

LUCA: When I was little

I would come down here for hours

All year round

Get down by the rocks

Trace my fingers along the lines

The ones I could reach

Then I would try to draw them later

When I got home

To see what I could remember

My family would laugh at me

So I would rush to my room

Place my finger tips on the paper

Pretend that they could draw

That the lines would draw themselves

As if they were part of me

Just me and the rocks

DOVE: They speak

Don't they?

LUCA: They've a lot to say

DOVE: That's a lovely story Luca

And now?

You still drawing the lines?

LUCA: Trying too

A murmuration of Starlings gathers. Takes flight. Lands. Catches the air. Startles **LUCA** *and* **DOVE**. *Catches and captures their imaginations. You can see it in their faces. You can hear the collective sounds of wings in motion. It is stark. Full of beauty. Unexpected. A moment of magic.*

DOVE: Starlings

LUCA: They're so playful

So free

DOVE: Moving like the echoes of a heart

LUCA: They know exactly who they are

DOVE: Summer's leaving us

Saying goodbye you fools

Until next time

We're off to another hemisphere

LUCA: I love the way they take flight

Catch waves of energy

DOVE: You can see they're listening to one another

LUCA: Why can't humans be more like that?

DOVE: You're thinking about the flag

LUCA: Its made me so sad

I don't know what to do

DOVE: We all need time to let it sink in

　　Be kind to ourselves

　　One another

LUCA: Can I ask you something?

DOVE: Of course

LUCA: Do you like being queer?

　　DOVE *laughs. It is hearty. Throws* **LUCA***.*

LUCA: Have I offended you?

DOVE: Had no idea what you were going to ask me

LUCA: Sorry

DOVE: No need to be

　　I'm still making a relationship with the word queer

　　Still trying to navigate its path for me

　　Doesn't mean I don't feel its presence

　　Its power for other people

　　Such a potent word for some

　　My generation

　　The abuse it contained

　　Caused a lot of shame

　　Pain

　　Loneliness

　　Was such a slur

　　I love who I am now

　　I love being gay

　　What it has brought to my life

Even the challenges

Took time to get there

To understand it

Felt uncomfortable

In the pit of my stomach for so long

When I didn't have any words

Couldn't speak it publicly

Own it with pride

Got buried for a long time

Before I found its joy

LUCA: I'm struggling

To find the right words

DOVE: Silence can be a dark place

> **LUCA** *buries their attention in their sketchbook.* **DOVE** *doesn't disturb the moment for them.*

LUCA: I come out here

So I don't just sit in my bedroom

Fester

Feel alone

Have to get away from home

Hard to leave it somedays

Harder during lockdown

I lost something during that time

It's like

I'm physically learning to lift myself up again

DOVE: I can relate to that

LUCA: I've got so used to being lit up

By the glare

Glow of a screen

Messages flashing

Filtering in

Soft pinging sounds

That in the end pierce

I put things on silent

Sometimes I'd just sit there

Staring at my phone

Wondering who to contact

Who to reply to

Seeing the messages

Feeling the love from my friends

I just can't always respond

Like it's all too much

Shadows of expectation everywhere

Can't escape them

Can't seem to switch off

Crazy isn't it?

DOVE: We all linger in those spaces for too long

Knowing how unhealthy it can be

Can also be a lifeline

Imagine growing up without the internet

LUCA: I can't

DOVE: We did

LUCA: How did you meet people?

DOVE: We found ways to connect

Discover who we were

It can be easier in cities

Networks form in their DNA

It's more difficult here I know

Distance from people who are the same

Access to support

It won't always be like this

There will be joy Luca

LUCA: As I peer into portals

Inviting me

Telling me

How to live

How to be

What to aspire to

I struggle to see myself

I rarely if ever see myself

DOVE: What do you want Luca?

LUCA: I want to be in the world

To contribute

Do something about the environment

Our planet

It frightens me

Feels so beyond my control

I don't know where to start

There's so much hatred out there

What kind of future does my generation have?

DOVE: I can't answer that

I wish I could

LUCA: There are so many demands

I can feel the edges of this place today

They're sharp

Close to collapsing

What we have built together

As a group

Suddenly we're standing on a cliff's edge

Four

VALENTINE. *Alone. In the early hours fuck it kind of time. Weary. Waiting for the dawn to rise majestically before her. A bottle of whisky knocking around. A box of objects from the past sprawled out in front of her. A rawness to her as she speaks.*

VALENTINE: As I wait for the dawn

unable to sleep

there's a note rising

getting closer

a tidal wave

of sound

heading

towards me

ready to wash

me away

another note

lands

softer than before

trying to sooth me

I reach out for it

start to run

it passes

through me

I look back

over

my shoulder

to see

if there is

more sound

trying not to trip

not to fall

My dream

it's not new

only

this sound is new

what I see

is just a mass

a blur

behind me

full of knots

Sounds

rise

fall away

like atoms

of dust

as one note

strikes the other

start to

disentangle

I stop running

watching

this happen

my breath

heavy and thick

the small

of my back

a film of sweat

Something

touches

my shoulder

I fall

to the ground

all my bones

have left my body

I just collapse

fold in on myself

like I'm made

of fuzzy felt

I'm just a shell

no organs

not a thing

no heart to beat

no muscle

to tense

hold me together

there is nothing left

birds flock

above me

swoop in

land

cover me

until

I disappear

the melody

they bring

is the sweetest

I have

ever heard

My heart

is cracked

its chambers

unleashing

discordance

a beat

out of time

I wonder

what is

this rhythm

inside

of me?

I know what it is

it's shame

still carried

buried

after all

this time

The legacy

of Section 28

follows me

burns

in my throat

if I try

to speak

about it

my voice

vanishes

That law

left me

and

others

stranded

All the things

I was starting

to understand

about myself

captured

in another way

publicly

rhetoric

full of hate

full of lies

telling us

we had

no right

to happiness

to exist

my childhood

forged

in stone

cold legislation

School

became

insufferable

as my visible

queerness grew

I began

to see

teachers

were

frightened of me

Any chance

to shut me down

was taken

It's still raw

only now I see

how it must

have been

raw for some

of them too

I started

to hide away

there wasn't

any oxygen

at school

at home

I couldn't

breathe

That feeling

I'd always had

of wanting

to run

since

I was

a child

grew

I've held this

inside of me

for decades

The first time

I danced

with another woman

I didn't know

what to do

her hands on me

was a

revelation

a

revolution

VALENTINE *starts to move to music. Stuck in that moment in time. Dancing.*

Five

QUILL and LUCA walking together on the beach. The waves roll and roar then find calm. Feet on the edges of the shoreline moment. Sea cold enough wild enough to send chills into bones. LUCA collects shells.

QUILL: That roar

> Every time

> Catches me out

> If I stop

> Look

LUCA: I struggle

> If I don't get close to it

> Where sea meets sand

QUILL: I usually run along these intertidal zones

> Good for my mental health

LUCA: Alone yet not alone

> I love it for that

QUILL: It's been intense

> Hasn't it?

LUCA: The last meeting

QUILL: Heated

LUCA: We need you

QUILL: I need to calm down

> It can get weird

> What with Val being my boss as well

LUCA: Sometimes

I think about stealing away

From this place

To a city

Overwhelmed

By a different kind of noise

People in abundance

Surrounded by crowds

Blending in amidst a wash of colour

A different kind of motion

Not being recognised

On the street

Do you?

QUILL: All the time

A feeling of common ground. Safety in this for both of them. The sun sparkles on them on the water as sand glistens. There's a sea spray glow to them. Makes **LUCA** *more open.*

QUILL: It can be hard being out

Being visible

LUCA: Feels like

I'm in a constant cycle

Waiting to be accepted

QUILL: You're making big choices right now

Don't underestimate the pressure

LUCA: There are so many labels

So many ways to identify

I'm trying to land

Accept where I am on the alphabet

I'm not quite there yet

QUILL: This in-between time

It's unnerving

Exciting

A scruffy mix

Churning around inside your stomach

I remember it

Wasn't so long ago

I was your age

On the cusp of needing everything to fall into place

It will

LUCA: Doesn't feel like it

QUILL: You're doing so much

Reaching out to me

Part of a group

That's so positive

Took me years

To stop running from my truth

I was always hurtling

From one moment to another

As if speed

Distance

Would go faster than my thoughts

Faster than my heart

So I didn't have to listen to either

Then something just clicked

Fell into place

I started to accept my own beauty

My own possibilities

Embracing all the parts of me

Letting them all sit together

In harmony not tension

I found belonging in that

LUCA: Am I being impatient?

QUILL: It's a process

Being human

It doesn't stop

You will shine

Find your path

Shells picked up after being washed by the water. Looked at. Pocketed.

LUCA: My dad

He laughed

When he heard about the flag

Roared in my face

Took delight in it

QUILL: Luca that's rough

I'm so sorry

Is it safe?

LUCA: It's oppressive

He looms large

Dominates

Won't let me speak

Can't accept me

Can't figure me out

Focuses on my siblings

Lockdown was hard

I missed my friends so much

Stuck at home

Without them

Being watched all the time

Rejected in silence

Day after day

I retreated

Hid in the white noise

QUILL: Luca means light

Doesn't it?

LUCA: You noticed

QUILL: Of course I did

It suits you

Chosen names are vital

A lifeline

LUCA: I've tried to explain this

At home

Being non-binary

Tried to ask for my pronouns

My name to be used

It's so hard

Being erased

Finding the right words

It's a battle

Dad doesn't get that

It's not much to ask

Is it?

QUILL: No

LUCA: Then why does it hurt so much?

QUILL: Everyday there will be something

That tries to tell you

That you don't belong

That the world isn't built for you

It's an effort to see what you bring to the world

It will take time to reach this

So we have to fight

To be seen

To be heard

To get the support we need

To create safe spaces

For ourselves

Our community

Even with those we love

We're trying to live our lives

Just like everyone else

Cis straight people have no idea

LUCA: I'm caught on these waves

They never stop

These feelings never seem to stop

My anxiety

QUILL: Right now

You have an ocean

Inside of you

Calling out to you

Crashing around

On repeat

Ceaseless motion

There will be days of calm

LUCA: Dove says there will be joy

QUILL: Dove's not wrong

The tide catches up with them. Catches them out. Laughter. **LUCA** *starts to take their shoes and socks off. Feet in. Loves being in the water. The feel of it.*

LUCA: Feels so good

Shoes and socks off Quill

QUILL: No way

LUCA: Those toes are going in

No cheating

QUILL: Too cold for me

LUCA: Don't be silly

It's a low tide luck day

QUILL *let's go and joins* **LUCA**. *They take a moment. As long as it takes. Standing in the ocean looking out.*

QUILL: I'd forgotten how to enjoy this vastness

Thanks for inviting me

Reminding me

what's right in front of me

Six

Same day as **LUCA** *and* **QUILL** *meet. Evening.*

The sky is awash with pinks and blues. It is utterly glorious. **VALENTINE** *and* **DOVE** *sit together outside gazing at the burgeoning night sky. They are in* **VALENTINE**'s *garden. Mending fishing nets. Might be some wine being drunk making them glow.*

DOVE: You do this every week?

VALENTINE: Helps local fishing folk out

DOVE: What compelled you?

VALENTINE: Her name is Violet

DOVE: Well well

VALENTINE: It's been a long time

DOVE: Does Violet know that?

VALENTINE: She does

DOVE: Why haven't I met her?

VALENTINE: It's new

> **VALENTINE** *takes a moment with this feeling.*

DOVE: Do you ever think of moving away?

VALENTINE: There's the odd pang

Every now and then

City life

Lesbian groups

Marches

Clubs

Pubs

Half of them gone

Knocked down

Gentrified

Homogenised

Heteronomatised

Apartmentasised

That's a word now by the way

Those places were community hubs

Saved lives

D.I.Y culture

Friday nights at First Out

That place has gone

Gutting

I remember queues for the loos

In the basement

Always took so long

Smoking cigars

Rebel dykes

Beautiful butches

There was a lot of leather in those days

DOVE: Your eyes are misting over

It's scaring me

VALENTINE: It was scary as fuck

Sexy too

Don't you remember the men in leather?

DOVE: Fondly

They were magnificent

They sit in that moment reminiscing.

VALENTINE: Do you want to meet someone new?

DOVE: Thought of it terrifies me

Dating apps don't appeal

VALENTINE: Not even to hook up?

DOVE: Do you mean for sex?

VALENTINE: I do

DOVE: I'm not ready

VALENTINE: Give me that

   DOVE *hands* **VALENTINE** *a corner of the net. They stretch it out. Take a look.*

VALENTINE: You missed a bit

DOVE: Must be the wine

Who'd have thought we'd be doing this

Me in my retirement

Very glamorous

VALENTINE: Do you miss it?

DOVE: Nursing?

It was a calling

Helped me make a difference

To all those who needed it

Sometimes I wake up

Ready to go to work

Then I remember

There's nothing

Staring back at me

Not even a dent on the other side of the bed

VALENTINE: Dove

DOVE: Tell me about your day

Please

VALENTINE: Talked to the press

DOVE: Taken them a while

VALENTINE: Not a feel good story

DOVE: Don't give them any credit

Our stories matter

Puts you in a spotlight

VALENTINE: It's necessary

DOVE: You have a very public job

VALENTINE: Which is why

I'm very happy to be

A very public lesbian

DOVE: You sure?

VALENTINE: It's my responsibility

DOVE: When are you going to share it?

VALENTINE: Thought you didn't want to get involved in that way

DOVE: I don't want to be interviewed by the local paper

Quill and Luca might

There might be other folk out there

VALENTINE: What do you suggest?

DOVE: The group needs more support

Let's think about that

Look this is important to me

Distracts me

Gets me out of the house

Your persistence

I mean it's annoying

VALENTINE: We need to be united

If we aren't

Then we're fucked

Need to support Luca and Quill more

It's messy out there

Rights being eroded

They're facing all kinds of things we didn't

Although I feel a sense of deja-vu

The world is so divided in all kinds of ways

I can't bear knowing all the statistics about

Homophobic and transphobic bullying in schools

Young people

At the very beginning of their lives being taunted

Living in fear

Feeling like they don't belong

It's shocking

Words have impact

They cause shame

Harm young souls

It's a lonely place

They need to be loved

Heard

Valued

DOVE: Loneliness is full of shame too

A moment between them. Letting silence linger.

VALENTINE: We're losing Quill

DOVE: He's disappointed

Give him some time

He'll come round

VALENTINE: I hope so

DOVE: You two like to spar

VALENTINE: He's so bright

Feels the world so differently to us

DOVE: They both do

They focus on the nets for a moment.

DOVE: Police have any idea who did it?

VALENTINE: Nothing yet

DOVE: You're hiding something

VALENTINE: I'm not

DOVE: You are

I know now when you are

Tell me

VALENTINE: When we announced the flag

I got some surprising mail

DOVE: What?

VALENTINE: Pathetic threats

DOVE: A threat isn't pathetic Valentine

What did they say?

VALENTINE: That they'd stop me

DOVE: You never said anything to anyone?

VALENTINE: Police know

DOVE: Bloody hell Val

VALENTINE: Those who did it will get bored

Move on to their next target

They want to antagonise

Bully

Frighten

I'm not frightened

DOVE: The problem now is that the threat isn't so visible

You used to see the fuckers coming

I worry about you

VALENTINE: Don't

DOVE: Are those folk still hanging around

Outside the library

When you work late?

VALENTINE: Not in a while

DOVE: Call me Valentine

I mean it

VALENTINE: I will

DOVE: I can drive you home

VALENTINE: Got my bike

DOVE: Is that wise?

VALENTINE: I always cycle

Unless there's a hurricane

DOVE: I could follow you

VALENTINE: You will not

I don't need your headlights spotlighting my arse

For everyone to see

DOVE: Hopeless

VALENTINE: There's been far more positive mail sent

DOVE: You still need to take care

VALENTINE: I don't want Quill and Luca to know

They've got enough going on

DOVE: If it escalates

I want to know

VALENTINE: I'll tell you

There is a moon now shining brightly in the sky. It dazzles. Feels otherworldly. A perfect harvest moon.

VALENTINE: Look at that

DOVE: Harvest moon

You don't see them like that very often

VALENTINE: Looks like it has landed on the sea

DOVE: Luminous loveliness

VALENTINE: It's so bold

I love bold

DOVE: You have to let people help you

It's painful for **VALENTINE** *to register this. She does.*

VALENTINE: I never got to tell my Mum

Who I was

Before she died

That tiny piece of legislation

When I was young

Those paragraphs

That rattled through our lives

When we were at the beginning

When I was at the beginning

There's a little piece of me

Still wanting to tell her

Decades later

Me still not quite finding the words to speak

DOVE: Oh Val

VALENTINE: I've been alone

For a long time

Sorry

DOVE: Don't be sorry

Just be more open

People care about you

A moment. **VALENTINE** *having to listen. To hear this.*

DOVE: Why has it been such a long time?

VALENTINE: You're relentless

DOVE: I'm not giving up

VALENTINE: I got my heart flattened

>Utterly flattened

>So I packed it away

>The ventricles

>Atriums

>Aorta

>Its linings

>The muscle walls

>All of it

>I hid it away

>So no one could find it

>*A tenderness between them as they pass things between them for the nets.*

DOVE: So what's next?

VALENTINE: I have an idea

DOVE: Are you going to share?

VALENTINE: You'll have to wait

DOVE: Waiting is horrible

VALENTINE: All will be revealed

Seven

Following week.

Library. **LUCA**, **VALENTINE** *and* **DOVE** *already there.* **QUILL** *arrives last.*

There are still tensions bubbling away underneath the surface.

What is left of the flag has been framed by **VALENTINE** *and is on display for them to see.*

VALENTINE: You're here

QUILL: You're nothing but true to your word

VALENTINE: Council don't approve

QUILL: Why would they?

VALENTINE: Told me to take it down

DOVE: It's still evidence

VALENTINE: Too provocative

DOVE: Might encourage further aggression

VALENTINE: They understand our feelings

QUILL: Your feelings

> **VALENTINE** *has to register this sentiment.*

VALENTINE: My feelings

> I thought
>
> I was reclaiming it
>
> Being a bit punk
>
> Instead
>
> I've caused more hurt

QUILL: Finally

DOVE: Clouds parting

VALENTINE: It's not a joke

   I want to tear it all down

DOVE: We understand that

VALENTINE: Do you?

DOVE: It's not helpful

VALENTINE: Then what do I do with this?

DOVE: Keep it safe

VALENTINE: Hidden you mean

   Like so much of our lives

   I'm too old now to live like that

   I can't

   I won't

DOVE: It's not exclusive to you that feeling you know

VALENTINE: I know

DOVE: Do you?

QUILL: This was traumatic for us Val

   You have to see that

   Accept it could be traumatic for you too

   They attacked us all

   We're vulnerable

   You're vulnerable

VALENTINE: What I am is furious

QUILL: Don't think I'm not angry too

LUCA: We're all angry

VALENTINE: We have to stand up to hate

I refuse to let this destroy the pride we felt

DOVE: Stop being such a warrior

VALENTINE: Really?

DOVE: I'm concerned

For your wellbeing

VALENTINE: Is this some kind of intervention?

DOVE: You're over reacting

A tinge of hurt lurking in the background. Silence. It's a make or break moment. **VALENTINE** *fighting hard to take stock. Reflect not react. She breathes deeply.*

VALENTINE: I dreamt about a pride event

A parade next year

They matter

I thought it could matter here

QUILL: Honestly

It scares me

When you say something like that

Even entertaining it

The idea of a pride parade

It's too big a leap

DOVE: We need to make decisions together

LUCA: It was the first time

I was visible

Publicly out to everyone

That meant so much

To stand side by side with you all

As I begin to accept who I am

Then bang

Everything crashing down

VALENTINE: Sorry Luca

I'm just compelled

DOVE: To be totally on your own trip?

Finally a little window of blue sky. **VALENTINE** *loosening.*

VALENTINE: I was going to say

To fight back

I can't help how I feel

My own trip

Noted

DOVE: Let's go gently

Steady ourselves

We're still reeling

VALENTINE: This arrived today

VALENTINE *places a package amongst them. She has already seen what's inside.*

LUCA: What is it?

VALENTINE: Take a look

LUCA *tentatively opens the parcel. Takes a look.*

LUCA: It's a new flag

DOVE: Who sent it?

VALENTINE: A gift

QUILL: From who?

VALENTINE: Anonymous

DOVE: Was there a note?

LUCA: "You're not alone

> You are valued

> We stand beside you

> Raise the flag

> We support you

> Lesbian

> Gay

> Bisexual

> Transgender

> Queer

> Intersex

> Asexual plus

> You are all a valued part of our community

> In solidarity"

> *Stunned silence.*

DOVE: Think I needed to hear that

LUCA: So did I

VALENTINE: Allies

QUILL: In an ideal world

> We'd put this up

VALENTINE: I could talk to the council

> Suggest some possibilities?

LUCA: February

> LGBT History Month?

Gives us time

DOVE: We would need assurances from them

    For our safety

    It's their job to support us

QUILL: Still feels too soon

VALENTINE: I would do it now

    Make a statement

    Raise the new flag

DOVE: Without permission?

LUCA: What if it happens again?

    Not sure I could take it

VALENTINE: It's an expression of who we are

QUILL: I get that

    I accept that

    Just so much focus on it

    I said it before

    Why place all our hope in one thing?

VALENTINE: Then we find another way

DOVE: Slow down

    Take stock

    Get more people interested in the group

QUILL: Are we underestimating

    the amount of queers

    around here?

VALENTINE: If we don't try

LUCA: Young people are scared

Sensitive about coming out

Joining a group

It's difficult

If their parents don't know

Public transport is so limiting

Not everyone has privacy

at home either

QUILL: Luca's right

It's difficult

DOVE: What about allies?

We clearly have them

QUILL: We can always do with more of those

VALENTINE: Who aren't anonymous

QUILL: It's tough

Travelling miles for an event

The separation that follows

Distance matters

LUCA: It's been a nightmare

During this time

Worse than before

College online

Friends far away

So much separation

VALENTINE: There just aren't the resources

I wish there was more to offer younger people

It's why solidarity

Allyship is so vital

DOVE: We were well supported for the raising of the flag

QUILL: I'm fed up of feeling like I'm fighting all the time

Fed up of all the obstacles

Aren't you?

VALENTINE: I'm exhausted

QUILL: That's a start

Something gives to allow for something more gentle to rise up around them.

LUCA: We had quite a crowd

Remember

When the flag was raised

DOVE: Weather was warm

VALENTINE: Sea was warm that day

No wetsuit to untangle myself from

DOVE: I never want to see that

VALENTINE: Quite a feat

LUCA: My friends were there

Yours were too Quill

QUILL: My Mum and Dad

LUCA: Wearing rainbow colours

QUILL: Don't remind me

DOVE: Landlord of my local pub joined us

VALENTINE: Those Sunday lunches paid off

DOVE: A moment of real joy

LUCA: I felt really proud to be there

VALENTINE: Our first action

LUCA: Together

DOVE: I remember thinking

It's a huge step

LUCA: Wanting the town

Our town

To see us

To really see us

That was huge

QUILL: My face hurt from all the smiling

LUCA: A sea of faces watching us

Hands clapping as Quill raised the flag

VALENTINE: The mayor's face

DOVE: She was pretty chuffed

Her chains glinting

VALENTINE: She was sweating in the heat

Everyone else was in short sleeves

T-shirts

Shorts

Very casual

LUCA: Then the choir

QUILL: I'd forgotten the choir

LUCA: I loved that they sang for us

QUILL: Their voices

    Carried across the square

DOVE: Towards the ocean

QUILL: Unfurling to the beat of the ocean

DOVE: The flag was caressed by a gentle breeze

QUILL: Midday sun

VALENTINE: Catching us all unaware

    Burning bright

LUCA: As we posed for the local paper

DOVE: Luca sketching

LUCA: It was like time stood still

They all stop still as if they are back there. Imagining the moment all over again. Dreaming it again. Swelling with pride. Together. We really see them as a group in this moment.

Solidarity returning.

VALENTINE: I found this photograph

    Fell out of a book I was restoring

    From a donated collection

    Landed at my feet

    Was staring right at me

    VALENTINE *shows them a photograph. They pass it between them.*

LUCA: Says 1923 on the back

DOVE: Beautiful handwriting

QUILL: Nightingale and Jack

VALENTINE: Look at them

    Locked in sepia

Grinning wide grins

Arms wrapped firmly around one another

QUILL: Their bodies completely at ease

VALENTINE: Faces from the past

QUILL: Reaching out

DOVE: They're in love

VALENTINE: Openly in this photo

QUILL: Who were they?

LUCA: Which one is Nightingale?

QUILL: Which one is Jack?

LUCA: They look gender non-conforming

VALENTINE: You're the historian amongst us Quill

QUILL: Who are they?

VALENTINE: Look at the cottage

QUILL: Rose cottage

VALENTINE: Recognise it?

LUCA: It's the one boarded up

Near the coastal path

QUILL: If we have a house

DOVE: We have a record

QUILL: Of lives lived

DOVE: Buildings tell stories

VALENTINE: They certainly do

QUILL: Did they rent it?

Did they own it?

In 1923 not everyone could own property

VALENTINE: Some things haven't changed

DOVE: Val

QUILL: What was their class?

DOVE: Nationality

QUILL: Ownership will tell us

VALENTINE: I've walked past there

  So many times

  It's a ghost

QUILL: Certainly has a ghostly presence

VALENTINE: Where were they from?

LUCA: Were they born here?

DOVE: What did they do?

QUILL: Who took the photograph?

DOVE: Did they have a community of friends?

VALENTINE: Visitors

QUILL: There's a rich heritage of queer artists

  Writers in the South West

  The book it fell out of

VALENTINE: Poetry collection

QUILL: Who wrote it

VALENTINE: Judith Edwards

QUILL: Could Judith be Jack?

DOVE: Is there an inscription?

VALENTINE: You read it Quill

QUILL: "For my darling Nightingale

My own constellation

Love Jack"

Palpable excitement in the air. It's welcome. Overwhelming.

VALENTINE: Could we create our own archive?

Inspired by this image?

Create a community around it?

QUILL: Let's where it leads us

VALENTINE: Us?

QUILL: Don't ruin it

I know what you're doing

VALENTINE: My heart just did a little dance

QUILL: Stop it

LUCA: Stories that matter

To us

VALENTINE: A living heritage

On our door step

LUCA: Something to celebrate

QUILL: Didn't see that coming

DOVE: It's not a bad idea

QUILL: No

It's a great idea

Eight

A few days later.

QUILL *is teaching* **VALENTINE** *some boxing basics. They are outdoors in a grassy field. Autumnal sunshine filters through and hits their bodies.* **QUILL** *has been showing* **VALENTINE** *how to do some boxing drills.*

VALENTINE: If those are the basics

    I'm fucked

QUILL: Valentine

    Breathe

    No heart attacks

    Drink something

VALENTINE: Give me water to swim in any day

QUILL: Are you giving up?

VALENTINE: Do you know me?

QUILL: Just a little

VALENTINE: I said I would give it a go

QUILL: Practice

VALENTINE: Show me again

    QUILL *demonstrates.* **VALENTINE** *follows. Slowly.*

VALENTINE: You make it look effortless

QUILL: Feet apart

    At an angle

    So you can bounce

    Defend

Watch me

QUILL *demonstrates another quick basic drill.*

QUILL: Remember you have a lead side

VALENTINE: And a rear side

QUILL: You were listening

VALENTINE: Cheeky

QUILL: Dominant hand

Your right one

Left foot forward

Use your hands

Protect yourself

Then you jab

Move your feet

Your weight

Good

Repeat

Hands

In front of your face

Protect it

Concentrate

VALENTINE *concentrates. Adjusts her posture. Thinks. Moves. Punches with more conviction this time. Almost enjoying it.* **QUILL** *hands her a towel.*

QUILL: Better

All about focus

VALENTINE: Enough

I'm literally throwing in the towel

For today

QUILL: Expecting more sessions?

VALENTINE: Coach Quill

QUILL: I like it

VALENTINE: I can tell

Laughter. Understanding amidst everything. Friendship.

QUILL: I wanted to be a boxer

When I was very young

I remember seeing two men

Fighting on TV

I loved their bodies

Their elegance

Roughness

Sweat pouring off them

My Dad is a big fan

I would sit with him at the weekend

Watch a fight

Learn its language

with him guiding me

Sharing his passion for it with me

I loved those afternoons

They lit me up

We used to spar

at home

He encouraged me

Play fighting

from an early age

In the playground

If they took the piss

I would punch them

Square in the face

Always ready for a fight

Something else inside of me

No language for it

Curled it up

Like two fists

at loggerheads

Everyday

I fought

and fought

Struggled

to keep momentum

Until night arrived

Me alone

in my room

Finally able

to be the boy

nobody else could see

I would dream about him

Long into the night

Morning breaking the spell

Breaking my heart

VALENTINE: There's so much I don't know

Quill?

What is it?

Caution in the air. **QUILL** *does have something on his mind.*

QUILL: I have to take flight

VALENTINE: You're leaving us?

QUILL: I will be

VALENTINE: When?

QUILL: Spring

VALENTINE: Why?

No

It's your business

QUILL: I need my trans siblings

My chosen family

I left behind

after university

I miss their buzz

I miss them

My heart longs for them

VALENTINE: Oh Quill

QUILL: I needed to accept myself here

To live openly as myself

Where I was born

Just for a while

In the place

where I sensed

hostility

for the first time

At the school gates

In the playground

VALENTINE: Brave doesn't cover it

QUILL: Honestly

There's been

more acceptance

than I thought possible

My parents have been amazing

I just need more

To be able to talk to trans friends

who understand

daily occurrences

micro aggressions

Other ways of being looked at

People who feel it too

In person

Not via a phone

That contact

That touch

I need it

VALENTINE: Not some grumpy old lesbian

who swears too much

QUILL: It's not all about you

Laughter. Liquid and warm.

VALENTINE: You're a beautiful person Quill

You've taught me a lot

QUILL: You're upset

VALENTINE *is visibly upset. She'll calm down.*

VALENTINE: I'll get over it

QUILL: You gave me a job

When others wouldn't

Showed me care

I'll never forget that

Although now

you've confused me

about leaving

Bringing the archive

into the mix

It's what I've always

wanted to do

You knew that

Saw that

Didn't you?

VALENTINE: I saw how much you cared

About stories from the past

QUILL: It's so exciting

Thinking about

discovering queer and trans stories

Illuminating lives

lost in time

To get to the heart

of someone

What made them tick

How they faced the world

Looked it in the eye

Stood up to it

Stories that would never be told

Searching for clues

That makes me so happy

To be able to do something about this

Change the narrative

Make a dent in the negativity

Push against the grain of mis-information

There's so much of it out there

About our lives

About being trans

Or non binary

Intersex

Queer

People know so little about us

We were always here

A constellation of hearts

Beating around the world

Hearts full of longing

Full of love

Did I just come out as a wanna be archivist and writer?

VALENTINE: You did

QUILL: My heart is so full

It wants to belong

To sing in a way

I haven't

in a long time

It wants to find

beauty

in numbers

in a crowded bar

pulsing with energy

To argue

late into the night

Dance

late into the night

Love

late into the night

That's what I want

I just needed to be ready

to go back

I am now

I love this place

It's helped

me grow

My family here

VALENTINE: Who adore you

QUILL: Who've got my back

It's gonna be hard

to leave them

I never told you this

The library

was a refuge for me

as a teenager

Had my corner

could curl up in that

window seat

dive into a book

escape the world outside

Rainy days

were the best

I would watch the steam rise

on window panes

as my imagination leapt around

There's so much to reach for

VALENTINE: You've been restless for a while

Then the flag

QUILL: It unnerved me more than I could have imagined

I was shocked by that

By how much I actually cared

I started to spiral

I was disappointed

VALENTINE: I felt that too

QUILL: I want to find my place

VALENTINE: You will

Lead on this Quill

If you want to

If you can

QUILL: I assumed you would

VALENTINE: I need to get out more

Go on dates

QUILL: I approve of that

VALENTINE: Write that book you've always aspired to

QUILL: Let's not get ahead of ourselves

VALENTINE: No pressure

QUILL: What about you?

VALENTINE: I came here to settle down

Whatever that means

I ended up having a relationship

with a library instead

QUILL: Well I'm glad you did

Better get on with the research then

VALENTINE: Maybe I'll learn how to punch before you go

QUILL: You got the rage

VALENTINE: I got the rage

I'll miss you

QUILL: I'll miss you too

Laughter and sadness in a delicate mix floats on the air. There is change ahead.

QUILL: C'mon

Up you get

One more drill

I'll be gentle

VALENTINE *groans feigning unwillingness. They gently spar at a distance. Swirling around lost in these thoughts only of the body and its currents and movements.*

Nine

Late winter. Cusp of Spring.

It's a murky day outside. A day where you have to combat the crushing feeling of darkness and dampness. Moods that lie ahead.

DOVE, **VALENTINE**, **LUCA** and **QUILL** *in the library. New flag is present. It is* **QUILL***'s last meeting before he leaves.*

VALENTINE: No speeches

DOVE: Really?

VALENTINE: Not by me

QUILL: I'll be back

DOVE: Speeches then

VALENTINE: When we launch the archive

LUCA: It's your last meeting

QUILL: No speeches

    Let's focus on

    Nightingale and Jack

    QUILL *lays out in front of them sheets of paper. Research. Images.*

LUCA: Rose Cottage needs some love

    In the photo it's so alive

    I imagine the gardens were once beautiful

    Abundant

    Bursting with colour

    It's so overrun now

QUILL: Be difficult to get inside

VALENTINE: Would be great though

DOVE: If it's safe

VALENTINE: We could try

DOVE: What?

VALENTINE: To break in

    In my dreams

    That's what we're doing

DOVE: You're hopeless

    DOVE *throws something at her. Warm exasperation.*

LUCA: Following the track

    From cottage

    to coastal path

    Knowing

    they would have

    walked all along

    this coastline

    Just blows my mind

QUILL: Queer and trans ancestors

    Right on our doorstep

    Often wondered what it would feel like

    To find something like this

VALENTINE: Tell us what you've found

QUILL: According to official records

    Judith Edwards and Clara Sylvia Wade

    lived at Rose Cottage for over twenty years

From just after the first world war

The house was owned by Judith's family

who originated from the South West

Judith is Jack

Clara

Nightingale

A poet and a painter

Story goes that they met in London

At an exhibition of Nightingale's paintings

in an underground club in Soho

known as The Cave

Abstract portraits of writer's

All very bohemian

Portraits expressive

of sexualities

gender non-conformity

It was quite a collection

No one seems to know

what happened to it

I suspect

it got dispersed

between the subjects

To keep their privacy

Their secrets safe

Clara signed her work

Nightingale

Another form of secrecy perhaps

Something she never

stopped doing

I like to think that Jack

was upset not being part

of this collection

Demanded a portrait

which was

the beginning

of their relationship

Jack was prolific as a poet

between the wars

Publishing with Hogarth Press

That belonged to Leonard and Virginia Woolf

I'd like to imagine the Woolf's visited

Rose Cottage

That they were here

There were an abundance of visitors

over the years

Feels like it was a sanctuary

It appears that their idyll began to fracture

as the second world war broke out

Nightingale was a pacifist

Openly anti-war

Both had marched on anti-fascist demo's

in the 1930s

Here and in Europe

They also went dancing

Had elaborate wardrobes

Jack wore masculine attire

Nightingale a mixture

Jack wanted to find a way to contribute

in the great war

She or they however you want to interpret Jack

Driving ambulances on the front line

So back to London in 1940

to drive on the night watch

Nightingale reluctantly returning

Clearly wanting to remain at Jack's side

Her instincts telling her they mustn't go

She was right

Jack was tragically killed

during an air raid in the Blitz

Gets a bit blurry after that

Nightingale was unable to stay in the cottage

Whether this was grief

or Jack's family

I don't know

She returned to America

after the war ended

Staying another three years

I can't seem to find out much

about this time

The Edwards family had money

Privilege and status

Enough to want to hide

a transgressive relative

and their lover

Or lovers as Jack had a reputation

Nightingale too

They could have been polyamorous

Jack's poetry hints at this

The family has an archive

Letters

Photographs of inside Rose Cottage

Not easy to get access to

This is an Edwards library isn't it?

I'll let you fill in the gaps there Val

Nightingale left a legacy of work

Now housed in an American University

Who also catalogued her surviving paintings

You can see some of them online

I'm just scratching the surface

Something happens in the air. It changes. Is full of electricity.

VALENTINE: Unbelievable work Quill

DOVE: You've done so much

QUILL: I had some help

LUCA: Sent me in all kinds of directions

    I loved finding these echoes

    Helping Quill conjure

QUILL: I tried not to take too many leaps

    Would be easy to do

DOVE: I loved the leaps

VALENTINE: I can't begin to wrap my head

    around Jack's family

    Having a stake in this building

    It's had so many lives

QUILL: They might

    Have stood

    Right here

LUCA: That's mad

DOVE: People come and go

    Leave us

    Leave imprints

    Make their mark

    Touch our lives

    Long after they are gone

VALENTINE: They do

DOVE: It's quite emotional really

QUILL: All from

    A photograph

    A book of poetry

    A patchwork of two lives

    Bound together

    By love

    By chance

VALENTINE: I think I need to lie down

QUILL: Not until we've thought about the rest of the archive

LUCA: Could we put in an object?

QUILL: I like that

    Places it

    Places us at its heart

DOVE: I'd be happy to do that

LUCA: Capture our lives now

QUILL: Queer culture is expansive

    I'd like to show that

LUCA: What else goes in an archive?

QUILL: Depends on the archive

VALENTINE: Notebooks

QUILL: Letters

DOVE: Love letters

VALENTINE: Diaries

    Postcards

DOVE: Poems

LUCA: Posters

VALENTINE: Fliers

QUILL: Zines

DOVE: Magazines

LUCA: Badges

VALENTINE: Pressed seaweed

DOVE: Who wants old seaweed?

VALENTINE: You'd be surprised

Capturing the smell of the sea from the past

DOVE: Sounds disgusting

VALENTINE: I think its romantic

QUILL: Like a queer ecology?

VALENTINE: Exactly

DOVE: Who would it be for?

VALENTINE: The seaweed?

DOVE: The archive

QUILL: We could discover that as we went along

LUCA: It would be for us

To begin with

VALENTINE: Then the wider community

QUILL: Especially with a local story

VALENTINE: The framed flag

Very recent history

LUCA: Could be part of an exhibition

DOVE: In the future

VALENTINE: That would get it back up on the wall

LUCA: I'd like a sense

of what is happening

in the wider world

DOVE: Go on Luca

LUCA: I mean barriers

Legal stuff

Gender recognition

Conversion therapy

DOVE: Can't believe we're still fighting these

LUCA: Social

Education

Healthcare

Environmental

VALENTINE: Be great if anyone had any banners from demo's

Past pride marches

DOVE: I have some ACT-UP posters

VALENTINE: Honouring our tradition of protest and activism

QUILL: Rallying cries of a united queerdom

DOVE: Were there police raids?

On local pubs hosting gay nights

Illicit knocks on doors

I'd love to know those things

QUILL: Statistics of hate crimes

might be interesting

DOVE: Weddings

   Civil partnerships

   Funerals

   I always feel like we're absent from cemeteries

   If we lived

   Then we died too

VALENTINE: I never thought of that

QUILL: We've looked back into the past

   Explored lives from a very particular background

   One more privileged than most

   Now let's make sure we also seek out

   voices and experiences

   beyond our own

   I would be interested in

   hearing those stories

VALENTINE: That's vital

QUILL: It has to be as expansive as possible

DOVE: Practical question

   Where's everything going to go?

VALENTINE: I thought your shed

   Perfect

DOVE: Very funny

   Mood edges into more serious territory. They know it's time for **QUILL** *to leave.*

QUILL: I have to go

VALENTINE: I don't like goodbyes

QUILL: It's only London

VALENTINE: Big place

DOVE: I don't miss it anymore

VALENTINE: Occasionally I do

DOVE: We'll be thinking of you

VALENTINE: Understatement

DOVE: We're good at that

LUCA: Can I visit?

QUILL: I'll be upset if you don't

Let me know

when you're

ready for launch

Wouldn't miss it

for the world

VALENTINE: We're relying on you to give a speech

QUILL: Done

> **QUILL** *leaves. They watch him walk away into the distance. Tiny heartbreak in the room.*

Ten

A leap in time. Summer is blossoming.

LUCA, **DOVE** *and* **VALENTINE**. *Summer. Outside. Sounds of people. The summer swell of bodies in a seaside town. Heat pushing through. They are eating ice creams.*

LUCA: Can't believe I moved out

Thank you for helping me

VALENTINE: Absolute pleasure

DOVE: How's the new job?

LUCA: I love it

Making coffee

Cocktails

Exhibiting my work

DOVE: That's so wonderful Luca

LUCA: I miss Quill

Didn't think I would

quite as much

DOVE: We all do

LUCA: He's so busy

VALENTINE: Working in an archive of all places

Love it

LUCA: Want to visit him

When I can

It's all got very full on

all of a sudden

Things opening up

New friends

DOVE: Old friends

VALENTINE: In need of ice cream

LUCA: I joined that beach clean up group

DOVE: Fantastic news

LUCA: I'm learning more about

how to protect

my immediate environment

VALENTINE: I can see it lights you up

DOVE: Perfect place to start

Then you can take on the world

LUCA: I stick with the archive work for now

I love it

Never thought

I would

Never thought

it could inspire so much

DOVE: It's surprised us all

LUCA: That photograph

VALENTINE: Who knew?

LUCA: You knew

VALENTINE: I had an inkling

LUCA: A gut feeling

DOVE: A new path

They all pause for a moment to consider this. Life. Movement. On.

LUCA: Hard to believe it's a year on

Since we raised the flag

DOVE: Anniversaries can sting

VALENTINE: We tried

DOVE: That's all that matters

VALENTINE: Good we're marking it

There's just one thing missing

LUCA: You mean one person

VALENTINE: I do

LUCA: He sent us a message

"You'll know when the time is right to try again,

With you in spirit

Raising the flag in our hearts

Love Quill."

VALENTINE: Can't argue with that

A moment for reflection.

VALENTINE: What else is new then?

LUCA: I'm learning to cook

VALENTINE: Do you like it?

LUCA: Might do a course

DOVE: Happy to be a test subject

LUCA: Early days Dove

VALENTINE: You've moved so far

LUCA: Quill helped me so much

Inspired me

To get on with things

I'm taking it slowly

Asserting my identity

as non-binary

at work

Feels right

It fits

DOVE: We're very proud of you

VALENTINE: Quill keeps sending me boxing links

Look at my right hook

DOVE: That's so funny

VALENTINE: I know

I'm a bloody librarian

for fuck's sake

Boxing

DOVE: You're branching out

VALENTINE: Letting go

LUCA: Me too

VALENTINE: Accepting help

LUCA: That's the big one

DOVE: Toughest one

VALENTINE: So true

DOVE: Took me ages to ask for help

VALENTINE: I'm working on it

DOVE: Are you?

VALENTINE: Stop it

    What about home Luca?

LUCA: I see my sister more

    She's cool

    Has a girlfriend

    Is planning on moving out

    Soon as she can

    Dad's furious

    We still don't really speak

DOVE: Maybe some distance will help

VALENTINE: One day he might see things differently

LUCA: I'm finding my feet

DOVE: More and more

LUCA: Every day

    Learning so much about myself

    Reaching out

    I contacted

    that young people's group

    Finally

    This place

    somehow

    held me together

VALENTINE: You did it Luca

LUCA: Doesn't mean everything

will always work out

Just feeling stronger

to face things

Must be the geology

or something like that

Holding things together

DOVE: Ancient lines

LUCA: Can't wait

for the archive

to launch

VALENTINE: We're almost there

LUCA: I've got something for you both

VALENTINE: Oh gifts

LUCA: I finally finished them

Finally felt I could

To say thank you

> **LUCA** *unpacks a bag with pictures in it they have drawn and painted of the day the flag was raised. Shares them.*

DOVE: I believe Valentine is a bit lost for words

Remember this moment Luca

It might not happen again for a while

They're stunning

I knew they would be

LUCA: Thanks Dove

For encouraging me

DOVE: Val

Are you crying?

VALENTINE: No

Yes

Of course I'm crying

you idiot

My heart is fit to burst

DOVE: Now these need framing

VALENTINE: Agreed

DOVE: For the launch

VALENTINE: Luca?

LUCA: Yes

Laughter permeates as they look at them and then in perspective of the town square where the library is and where the flag would have been raised.

VALENTINE: Any more surprises?

I might not cope

The warmth of their laughter flies through the air. Warmth not fear.

Eleven

Few months later.

It is a couple of days before the archive launch day and the group are meeting.

LUCA, **DOVE**, *and* **VALENTINE** *have parts of the archive in front of them. Working out how to display it and looking at objects.*

Everything is illuminated by hope and love. Let's not forget love's glow.

Then. It's **QUILL**. *Back with them. In front of them. Beaming in warm summer sun.*

QUILL: How's that right hook?

VALENTINE: Well I haven't tried it out on anyone

DOVE: Not yet

VALENTINE: The day is young

DOVE: Great to have you back Quill

Can't wait to hear your news

QUILL: Plenty to share

LUCA: We missed you

QUILL: We?

LUCA: I missed you

You look like yourself

QUILL: I feel like myself

So do you

LUCA: Val says I've grown

QUILL: I don't think she means in height

VALENTINE: You kept this quiet

LUCA: It wasn't easy

VALENTINE: We weren't expecting you for a few more days

QUILL: I couldn't wait

How's Quill's corner of books?

VALENTINE: Thriving

Can't quite believe how popular it is

LUCA: I've read most of them

VALENTINE: Might need some new titles

QUILL: I did spend a lot of time

hiding and reading

in that corner of the library

when I worked here

VALENTINE: It was noticed

LUCA: There's such a range of writers

James Baldwin

Juno Dawson

Thomas Page McBee

Kate Charlesworth

Maggie Nelson

Jackie Kay

Ocean Vuong

Kae Tempest

Sappho

Sarah Waters

Eileen Myles

Jack Halberstam

Radclyffe Hall

Audrey Lourde

Joelle Taylor

H.D

Shon Faye

to name a few

QUILL: How did you remember all of those?

DOVE: Youthfulness

VALENTINE: Not just for the young

DOVE: So true

LUCA: Less time online

More time reading

DOVE: One of life's great pleasures

VALENTINE: Quill's corner is here to stay

QUILL: Any seaweed been sent in for the archive?

VALENTINE: Not yet

*Laughter at **VALENTINE**'s desire for seaweed to be sent in.*

VALENTINE: You wait and see

Seaweed will have its day

The others laugh at Val's expense. Anticipation in the air.

LUCA: We could share our objects now Quill's with us?

Not sure I can wait

VALENTINE: No time like the present

Dove?

DOVE: I knew you'd say that

Alright

This is the invitation Hugh and I sent out for our wedding

Finally legal in 2013

Giving us rights

Protection under the law

A chance to celebrate our love with friends

Families

Those who were left

My father long dead

My mother elderly and excited

New found lease of life

We had this portrait of us taken

First time we had ever done anything like that

We were so proud of it

Standing side by side

Looking handsome as fuck

After all those years

We'd made a life together

Made a home

Made it work against so many odds

I know not everyone can get married

The law still has some lengths to go here

In other countries around the world where it's impossible

I also understand its not for everyone

Nor should it be

It was for us

Living through such times as we did

We felt like we'd made it

Hand in hand

Making vows we had written

Words for each other

Spoken softly

Amidst tears

It was a spectacular day

We danced so much

That day

It's etched on my heart

VALENTINE: You've not spoken about this before

DOVE: Felt right somehow

QUILL: You both totally look handsome as fuck

DOVE: No crying Val

VALENTINE: Who me?

QUILL: Better now than at the launch

VALENTINE: Can't guarantee it

DOVE: I'm glad I did

Haven't quite found the words

To talk about Hugh

VALENTINE: This is a good start

DOVE: Thank you

LUCA: Quill?

QUILL: I've brought this pin badge of the trans flag

A sign of solidarity

Visibility

I know I know

what I've said about flags

in the past

I feel the irony

It's created by a non-binary designer

Who is amazing

Given to me

by someone new in my life

Someone who has become special

I managed

to get another one

for the archive

It's pretty unique

A limited edition

Set in silver

I actually watched mine being made

Was there as it was born

Took me back

to new beginnings

Moments

of things being forged

in fire

LUCA: I want one

VALENTINE: It's gorgeous

DOVE: So delicate

VALENTINE: This someone special

QUILL: Val

VALENTINE: What?

DOVE: Save it for later

VALENTINE: I will

QUILL: Your turn

LUCA: Come on

VALENTINE: This was a tough choice for me

> So many objects collected over so many years
>
> Memorabilia if you like
>
> All of them telling my story
>
> My own archive
>
> A life in a box
>
> Took me back
>
> To being younger
>
> Tentative moments
>
> when I thought the world would cave in
>
> Collapse if I told anyone
>
> I was gay
>
> When I tried to fit in at a bar
>
> Which I often didn't
>
> Escaping home

Finding a bunch of misfits

to call my own

Owning my space

for the very first time

I haven't worn this

for a long time

A t-shirt

Integral to any movement

From the very first pride march I went on

In another century

First time I wore something like this

Out and proud

I wore it non stop afterwards

So everyone would know

Was a defining moment for me

Probably needs a wash

It's a bit musty

QUILL: I can smell it from here

VALENTINE: Adds something to the story

DOVE: Keep telling yourself that

VALENTINE: The words are fading

I fell in love

for the first time

wearing this

DOVE: Are you sure you want to donate this?

VALENTINE: Yes

It was a point in time

Luca?

LUCA *starts to set up a camera. They are all a bit emotional.*

LUCA: So I thought

We could capture this moment

Just the four of us

Before guests arrive

Before first night nerves

Us

Our small friendly group

A different kind of family portrait

Here in this public space

This shared space

we have

tried to make as safe

as we can

Where we gather

Together

Come on

DOVE: Haven't done my eyes

QUILL: You'll do

VALENTINE: I look like

I was dragged

out of a hedge backwards

DOVE: It's a look

VALENTINE: That's so rude

They are captured in this moment in time. Smiling. Together. Ready for the future.

DOVE: Look at us

LUCA: Do you like it?

DOVE: I love it

QUILL: We look gorgeous

DOVE: It's a keeper

VALENTINE: I want my own copy

QUILL: Me too

DOVE: Such a simple idea

VALENTINE: Our stories matter

Don't let anyone tell you differently

Images of Nightingale and Jack. Of the flag flying. Of the group as their objects light up the space and time. Together.

Twelve

LUCA steps out of the portrait and into a field full of wildflowers. Lit up with green carnations and violets. The sky is awash with pinks and blues. It is utterly glorious. It dazzles. Feels otherworldly. LUCA is utterly at home in it.

Music.

LUCA: I watch us

in this moment

our faces beaming

cracking

wide smiles

like sunshine

breaking

over waves

like dawn rising

parting

dark clouds

Our hearts

size of a fist

fit to burst

full of electricity

moving around

our bodies

racing in time

out of time

layers

of sound

not yet heard

words

not yet

uttered

declarations

not yet

made

These hearts

carry sadness

old wounds

new wounds

catching them out

under this

neon glow

hearts

often

weighted down

tearing

at night's blanket

Hearts

spun around

by doubt

fear

as the

world

crashes in

Sometimes

we are fragile

muted

drained

of colour

sometimes we

falter

stand still

wrestling with

passions

that rise

sometimes

courage

fails to

soar

Not tonight

tonight

these hearts

of ours

are

shining bright

tonight

we are

telling our

own stories

scaring

off shadows

harboured

from long ago

These are

hearts

that weather

storms

get seized

by

anger

frustration

hurt

Hearts

that are full

to the brim

with love

with hope

possibility

there are

rivers

of tenderness

running

through us

constantly

moving

and

changing

and

dancing

to the beat

of

our hearts

They are lit up. Making their own constellation. Their own night sky.

End.